THE ROYAL STORY

Written by Crystal J Williams

Illustrated by Carrie Collins-Whitfield

AuthorHouse™
1663 Liberty Drive
Bloomington, IN 47403
www.authorhouse.com
Phone: 1 (800) 839-8640

Published by AuthorHouse 04/02/2019

ISBN: 978-1-7283-0637-7 (sc)
ISBN: 978-1-7283-0638-4 (e)

Library of Congress Control Number: 2019903975

Print information available on the last page.

This book is printed on acid-free paper.

authorHOUSE®

THE ROYAL STORY

This Story takes place with the
First known Kings and Queens.

In the land of Alkebulan, Thousands of years ago. Kimmie asked Daddy to tell her more of the Kings and Queens of the Alkebulan Dynasty. This was the first continent on earth where Humans lived.

One Queen was Ank, She was of the Eighteenth Dynasty of Egypt. Queen Ank, was the third of six known Daughters, born to Pharaoh Akhenaten and Nefertiti.

The Queen Ank was married to the great King Tut. Then Kimmie turns to daddy, and said. I'm I Queen Kimmie? Am I the ruler of this house. I must have my royal things, so that you know I'm a Queen. Kimmie's Daddy say's, "Wait a minute, there's no way you can bypass being a princess first".

Kimmie says, "But daddy I WANT TO BE ONE NOW. Daddy says, "Ok let's pretend". "I have to find my royal clothing What should I wear Daddy?"

"We will use our mudcloth fabric, we'll wrap it around you like a dress.

This will be the royal dress. Kimmie asked, "Why are these colors on the mudcloth only black and white?"

Daddy says, Meaning "Earths is Mud, Lan means, (Fini), means cloth", from this we get the translation, Mud Cloth. Bogolan is easily confused with other folk dying techniques, such as batik or tie dye. Mud cloth is called Bogolanfini, we call it mudcloth.so that we are able to pronounce it. Kimmie. What's that pot doing on your head, Daddy asked Kimmie? This is my Royal Crown Daddy, now I need to find my Royal necklace.

"Daddy!! Daddy!! LOOK my teddy
bears are building my pyramids".

I found my Royal necklace it's cowrie shells,
now I'm ready to rule this house, I need juice
and a snack this queen is overdue a nap.

The end for now get ready for the
next Story issues, Guys..

Author Biography

Crystal Williams is 30 years of age. She owns a Business by the name of CW's Heal Thyself. She has two little ones with ages 8 and 6 and they always want to hear mommy's detailed imaginary entertaining stories. She tries to make learning fun for them with in the stories she tells them so that they are not just hearing a story, but also information about history.

She is very culturally inclined and enjoys learning new things. She knows that children enjoys a good story so she thought why not put the two together.

She grew up in Kansas City, Kansas and attended Hickman Mills High School. She have always been into fine arts. In high school, she took up drama, arts and enjoyed every part of it. She attended in Harris Stowe University and also Forest Park Community College in St. Louis Mo.

Printed in the United States
By Bookmasters